Smart Accounting with Tally: A Practical Approach

NotesKaro

Published by NotesKaro Inc, 2025.

SMART ACCOUNTING WITH TALLY: A PRACTICAL APPROACH

First edition. May 25, 2025.

ISBN: 979-8231187843

Written by NotesKaro.

Table of Contents

Chapter 1: Introduction to Accounting & Tally

A Humanized Start to a Digital Skill

In today's dynamic business world, every transaction, whether it's as small as purchasing a pen or as significant as acquiring a new office space, becomes a part of the company's financial story. And to manage this story with accuracy and efficiency, **Accounting** steps in as a backbone — not just of business, but of trust, regulation, and future planning.

But here's the catch — traditional accounting methods are time-consuming, error-prone, and, frankly, not suitable for today's fast-paced digital economy. This is where **Tally** becomes a game-changer.

Let's dive into this chapter not just to learn about accounting or how to use Tally, but to truly understand why mastering this tool is like learning the digital language of modern business.

1.1 What is Accounting?

Accounting is often called the "language of business" — and rightly so. It is the systematic process of recording, classifying, summarizing, analyzing, and interpreting financial transactions. The goal is to provide stakeholders like business owners, investors, tax departments, and management with clear, honest financial insights.

Key Objectives of Accounting:

- **Record-Keeping**: Keeping track of all business transactions.
- **Decision Making**: Helping managers plan budgets, manage cash flow, and make strategic choices.

- **Compliance**: Ensuring the company meets taxation and regulatory requirements.

- **Financial Reporting**: Communicating the company's financial health to shareholders, banks, or investors.

Types of Accounting:

- **Financial Accounting** – Prepares financial statements like Profit & Loss and Balance Sheet.

- **Management Accounting** – Used internally for decision-making and planning.

- **Cost Accounting** – Focuses on capturing the cost of production.

- **Tax Accounting** – Deals with income tax, GST, TDS, and other tax compliances.

1.2 Manual Accounting vs. Digital Accounting

Before software, accounts were handwritten in journals and ledgers. Errors were common, audits were lengthy, and scalability was poor. Now, digital tools have changed the game.

Aspect	Manual Accounting	Digital Accounting (Tally)
Accuracy	Error-prone	Highly accurate
Speed	Slow entry & calculations	Fast & automated
Audit Trail	Difficult to maintain	Easy to trace every entry
Reports	Prepared manually	Instant reports
Data Security	Paper-based, risky	Encrypted & backed up

1.3 What is Tally?

Tally (short for Transactions Allowed in a Linear Line Yards) is an accounting software used by businesses of all sizes. Developed by **Tally Solutions Pvt. Ltd.**, it is one of India's most trusted financial tools.

Key Features:

- User-friendly interface, even for non-accountants
- Handles multiple companies, currencies, and tax structures
- Real-time financial reports
- GST, TDS, Payroll integration
- Backup, restore, remote access

Fun Fact:

Over **2 million businesses** in India and beyond use Tally as their default accounting system.

1.4 Versions of Tally

Tally has evolved dramatically over the years:

- **Tally 4.5 (1990s)** – MS-DOS-based
- **Tally 6.3/7.2 (2000s)** – Added inventory and VAT
- **Tally 9** – Multi-lingual support
- **Tally ERP 9** – Introduced GST compliance, remote access

• **TallyPrime** – Latest version with modern interface, simplicity, and adaptability

If you're starting today, **TallyPrime** is your go-to version.

1.5 Why Tally is Essential for Business Students

Whether you're going to be a finance professional, a startup founder, or a freelancer, understanding accounting and Tally gives you a real edge.

Benefits:

• **Job-Ready Skill**: Over 80% of accounting jobs in India require Tally skills.

• **Confidence in Business**: Know where your money is going.

• **Better Internships**: Many SMEs and startups prefer Tally-proficient interns.

• **Freelance Projects**: You can offer bookkeeping services remotely.

Example: A B.Com student from Delhi learned Tally in his 2nd year. By 3rd year, he was managing 4 local shops' accounts and earning Rs. 10,000/month — while still studying.

1.6 Basic Terms to Understand Before You Use Tally

Let's simplify accounting lingo before we dive deeper.

• **Assets**: What your business owns (cash, machinery)

• **Liabilities**: What your business owes (loans, dues)

• **Capital**: Owner's money invested in the business

- **Revenue**: Earnings from sales
- **Expenses**: Costs to run the business
- **Ledger**: Account of a particular item (like Rent, Sales)
- **Voucher**: A document to record a transaction

1.7 Interface of TallyPrime: A Quick Tour

Once you install and open TallyPrime, the home screen shows:

- **Gateway of Tally** – The main menu
- **Company Info** – Create, select, or alter company
- **Chart of Accounts** – All ledgers, groups, cost centres
- **Transactions** – Record payments, receipts, sales, etc.

It's keyboard-friendly and supports mouse navigation too.

1.8 Tally for Students: Learning Path

Here's a smart roadmap to follow:

1. **Learn basics of accounting** (terms, principles)
2. **Install TallyPrime** (educational mode is free)
3. **Create a company** and practice ledgers
4. **Enter basic vouchers** like sales, purchase
5. **Add GST setup** and file returns
6. **Explore reports**: P&L, Trial Balance, GSTR
7. **Move to payroll, TDS, and MIS reports**

1.9 Practice Scenario: Let's Create a Mock Company

Company Name: Sunrise Stationery Pvt. Ltd.

Scenario:

- Capital Introduced: Rs. 1,00,000
- Bought Inventory (Pens, Notebooks): Rs. 30,000
- Sold Stationery worth Rs. 50,000
- Paid Rent: Rs. 5,000

Practice: Create ledgers, enter these transactions, and generate reports in TallyPrime.

1.10 Conclusion: Your Journey Begins Now

Accounting is not just for accountants anymore. Whether you're an entrepreneur, a freelancer, or a management student — understanding finances and being able to manage them digitally through Tally is a superpower.

Tally not only helps record numbers, but it teaches **discipline, analysis, and decision-making**, which are vital in every career.

Stay curious. Stay hands-on. Let's Tally your growth.

Chapter 2: Installing Tally Prime & Creating a Company

Tally Prime is a powerful accounting and business management software trusted by millions of businesses worldwide. Before diving into accounting functionalities, the first and most essential step is getting Tally Prime installed and setting up your company profile. In this chapter, we'll walk through the installation process, system requirements, and a step-by-step guide to creating your first company on Tally Prime.

1. System Requirements for Tally Prime

Before you install Tally Prime, ensure your system meets the minimum requirements:

Operating System: Windows 7 or higher (Tally is not natively available for macOS)

Processor: 1.8 GHz or faster (Dual-core and above recommended)

RAM: Minimum 2 GB (4 GB recommended)

Hard Disk Space: At least 150 MB of free disk space

Internet: Required for licensing and updates (Tally can work offline after setup)

Other: A PDF reader for printing invoices, and printer drivers installed (for invoice printing)

2. Installing Tally Prime

Step-by-step Installation Process:

1. **Download the Setup File:**

    ○ Visithttps://tallysolutions.com and download the latest Tally Prime version.

2. **Run the Installer:**

    ○ Locate the downloaded .exe file and double-click to run.

3. **Choose Installation Folder:**

    ○ By default, it installs in C:\Program Files\TallyPrime—you can change it as needed.

4. **Select Components:**

    ○ Select "TallyPrime Application" and proceed with installation.

5. **Installation Complete:**

    ○ Once installed, a desktop icon is created. Launch Tally Prime from there.

Tip: You don't need a high-end PC. Even a modest configuration can smoothly run Tally.

---

3. Activating License (Optional for Educational Use)

After installation, Tally Prime asks you to activate the license:

- **Full License:** For regular businesses (paid version)
- **Educational Mode:** Ideal for students and learning purposes (free)

If you're just exploring or learning, select "Educational Mode."

Note: In educational mode, you can enter data only for the 1st, 2nd, and 31st of each month.

4. Creating a Company in Tally Prime

To start working on accounts or ledgers, you must create a company. Here's how:

Step-by-Step Guide:

1. **Launch Tally Prime**

2. From the **Startup screen**, select Create Company

3. Fill in the following details:

    ○ **Company Name**: E.g., Galaxy Traders Pvt. Ltd.

    ○ **Mailing Name & Address**: This appears on all invoices.

    ○ **Country and State**: Important for GST & tax configuration.

    ○ **PIN Code, Phone, Email**: For records and communications.

    ○ **Financial Year From**: Usually starts from 1st April.

    ○ **Books Beginning From**: Usually the same as financial year.

    ○ **Security Control**: Set a username/password if multiple users are expected.

4. After filling in all details, press Ctrl + A to accept and save.

Congratulations, your company is now created!

5. Company Features Configuration

Post company creation, configure some features as needed:

- **GST Setup**: Go to F11 > F3: Statutory and enable GST.
- **Inventory Features**: Enable if your business deals in stock.
- **Payroll Feature**: Activate if managing employee salaries.

These features make Tally a complete ERP solution, not just an accounting tool.

6. Switching Between Companies

You can create and manage multiple companies in Tally Prime:

- Use Alt + F3 to open the company info menu.
- Choose Select Company to switch.
- Use Shut Company to close an active one.

Real Example: A freelance accountant managing 5 SMEs can keep separate data for each client securely.

7. Backing Up and Restoring Data

Data safety is crucial. Here's how to take backups:

- **Backup:** From Gateway of Tally > Alt + Y > Backup
- **Restore:** Use Alt + Y > Restore
- Store backups on cloud or pen drives regularly.

8. Common Errors and How to Avoid Them

- **Incorrect Financial Year:** Always double-check date entries.
- **Wrong State Setup:** Impacts GST calculations.
- **Company Not Opening:** Try using "Select Company" instead of "Create New" again.

Conclusion

Installing Tally Prime and creating a company might sound technical, but with these steps, even a beginner can set up the software without any help. Once this foundation is ready, you unlock the vast capabilities of Tally for accounting, inventory, payroll, taxation, and more.

Chapter 3: Understanding Ledgers & Groups

Tally Prime, like any efficient accounting software, is built upon the framework of ledgers and groups. These two components are the heart of Tally's double-entry accounting system. Without understanding ledgers and groups, one cannot fully utilize the software's potential or ensure accurate financial record-keeping. In this chapter, we will explore what ledgers and groups are, how they work in Tally Prime, and how they can be managed effectively.

3.1 What Are Ledgers?

A ledger is a principal book or computer file for recording and totaling economic transactions measured in terms of a monetary unit of account. In Tally, a ledger is where you record individual transactions relating to a particular account.

Example: If your company pays rent every month, you would create a ledger called "Rent Paid" under the group "Indirect Expenses."

Each ledger is associated with a group. Groups help in organizing the ledger accounts and in preparing financial statements such as the Profit & Loss Account and the Balance Sheet.

3.2 Understanding Groups in Tally

Groups in Tally are predefined categories under which ledgers are classified. Tally has 28 predefined groups, of which 15 are primary groups and 13 are sub-groups. Users can also create custom groups if needed.

Primary Groups Examples:

- Capital Account
- Loans (Liability)
- Current Assets
- Fixed Assets
- Sales Accounts
- Purchase Accounts

Why Groups Matter:

- They simplify report generation.
- They automate the classification of accounts.
- They help maintain consistency in bookkeeping.

3.3 Types of Groups

1. Capital and Liabilities:

- Capital Account
- Reserves and Surplus
- Loans (Liability)

2. Assets:

- Fixed Assets
- Current Assets
- Investments

3. Income:

• Sales Account

• Direct Income

• Indirect Income

4. Expenses:

• Direct Expenses

• Indirect Expenses

Note: Tally automatically places every ledger in a group, and the group determines how the ledger will be treated in financial reports.

3.4 Creating a Ledger in Tally Prime

Steps:

1. Gateway of Tally > Create > Ledger
2. Select the appropriate group
3. Enter the ledger name, opening balance (if any), and other details
4. Save the ledger

Example: To create a ledger for Electricity Bill:

• Name: Electricity Bill

• Group: Indirect Expenses

• Opening Balance: Nil (or past due if applicable)

3.5 Creating a Group in Tally Prime

Tally also allows users to create custom groups to better classify specific expenses or income sources.

Steps:

1. Gateway of Tally > Accounts Info > Groups > Create
2. Enter Group Name
3. Specify whether it is a Primary Group or a Sub-group
4. Assign the parent group

Example:

- Group Name: Online Marketing
- Under: Indirect Expenses

3.6 Altering or Displaying Ledgers and Groups

Sometimes, you may want to update or review the details of a ledger or group.

To Alter:

1. Gateway of Tally > Accounts Info > Ledgers > Alter

To Display:

1. Gateway of Tally > Accounts Info > Ledgers > Display

Use these functions to keep your records accurate and up-to-date.

3.7 Common Mistakes to Avoid

- **Misclassification:** Placing a ledger under the wrong group (e.g., placing "Salary" under Direct Expenses instead of Indirect Expenses).
- **Duplicate Ledgers:** Creating multiple ledgers for the same purpose due to naming inconsistencies.
- **Improper Naming:** Not using clear and identifiable names for ledgers (e.g., using "Bills" instead of "Electricity Bill").

3.8 Practical Use-Case

Scenario: You are running a small retail business and regularly make purchases from multiple suppliers and sell goods to various customers.

Suggested Ledgers & Groups:

- Supplier ABC: Sundry Creditors
- Customer XYZ: Sundry Debtors
- Rent: Indirect Expenses
- Bank of India: Bank Accounts

This helps you track receivables, payables, and regular expenses efficiently.

3.9 Importance of Proper Ledger & Group Management

- Enables easy audit and financial analysis
- Reduces time in generating reports
- Helps in accurate filing of GST and other compliances

3.10 Tips for Better Ledger & Group Usage

- Stick to a consistent naming convention
- Regularly review and clean up unused ledgers
- Train your team on group classification

Summary

Understanding Ledgers and Groups is crucial for any business using Tally Prime. This foundational knowledge sets the stage for accurate accounting, efficient reporting, and effective financial decision-making. A well-structured ledger and group system reflects the professionalism of your bookkeeping process and enables long-term financial clarity.

Chapter 4: Voucher Entries – Receipts, Payments, Contra, Journal

In the world of accounting, vouchers are documents that serve as proof of financial transactions. In Tally Prime, voucher entry is one of the most critical tasks, as it forms the foundation of recording business activities accurately. In this chapter, we will dive into the key types of vouchers – Receipts, Payments, Contra, and Journal – and understand how to record them efficiently with relevant examples.

Understanding Vouchers in Tally Prime

A voucher in Tally Prime represents a document used to record a financial transaction. Every transaction, whether it is related to cash, bank, or non-cash adjustments, is entered using a specific voucher type.

Tally Prime comes with predefined voucher types such as:

- Receipt Voucher (F6)
- Payment Voucher (F5)
- Contra Voucher (F4)
- Journal Voucher (F7)

Each voucher type serves a specific purpose, and choosing the correct one is crucial for accurate bookkeeping.

---

1. Receipt Voucher (F6)

Purpose: Used to record money received into the business from customers, cash sales, or income.

Common Scenarios:

- Customer pays an invoice amount.
- Interest income received.
- Capital introduced into business.

Example:

Your business receives Rs. 10,000 from a client, Mr. Sharma, for services rendered.

Steps to Record in Tally Prime:

1. Go to **Gateway of Tally > Vouchers > F6: Receipt**
2. Select the **Bank** or **Cash** ledger under 'Account' (where money is received).
3. Under 'Particulars', select **Mr. Sharma's Ledger**.
4. Enter Rs. 10,000 and provide narration like: *Being amount received against invoice #INV101.*

Tip: If you are receiving via cheque or bank transfer, ensure to select the bank account accordingly.

---

2. Payment Voucher (F5)

Purpose: Used to record all payments made by the business – expenses, loan repayments, purchases, etc.

Common Scenarios:

- Rent paid

- Salaries disbursed
- Supplier payment

Example:

You paid office rent of Rs. 15,000 in cash.

Steps to Record:

1. Navigate to **F5: Payment** from Vouchers menu.
2. Select **Cash Account** under 'Account'.
3. Under 'Particulars', choose **Rent Expense Ledger**.
4. Enter Rs. 15,000 and give a narration: *Rent paid for the month of April.*

Tip: Always ensure that the ledger you are debiting/crediting has the correct group assigned (like Expenses, Sundry Creditors, etc.)

3. Contra Voucher (F4)

Purpose: Used for transactions within cash and bank accounts of the same business. It does not affect income or expense.

Common Scenarios:

- Cash deposited into bank
- Cash withdrawn from bank
- Bank to bank transfers

Example:

Rs. 20,000 cash deposited into HDFC Bank account.

Steps to Record:

1. Select **F4: Contra** from the voucher menu.
2. In 'Account', choose **HDFC Bank.**
3. Under 'Particulars', select **Cash Account.**
4. Amount: Rs. 20,000 | Narration: *Cash deposited into HDFC Bank.*

Tip: Contra entries are internal transactions and must be marked accordingly in reports.

---

4. Journal Voucher (F7)

Purpose: Used to record adjustments that do not involve cash or bank – for example, depreciation, provisions, and corrections.

Common Scenarios:

- Depreciation of assets
- Rectification entries
- Accrued expenses or income

Example:

Charging depreciation of Rs. 5,000 on office equipment.

Steps to Record:

1. Go to **F7: Journal**.
2. Debit **Depreciation Account**.
3. Credit **Office Equipment Account**.
4. Amount: Rs. 5,000 | Narration: *Depreciation on office equipment for April.*

Tip: Journal vouchers should be reviewed periodically for correctness, especially for audit purposes.

Best Practices for Voucher Entry:

- Use proper narrations for clarity.
- Ensure ledgers are grouped correctly.
- Cross-check balances after every entry.
- Backup your data regularly.

Chapter 5: Sales & Purchase Entries

In any business, sales and purchases are the lifeblood of operations. Recording them accurately and efficiently is crucial for financial tracking, legal compliance, and strategic planning. In Tally Prime, Sales and Purchase Vouchers are designed to make this process smooth, structured, and detailed.

---

1. Understanding Sales Vouchers

Sales vouchers in Tally are used to record the sale of goods or services to a customer. It can be a cash or credit sale, depending on the mode of transaction.

Types of Sales:

- **Cash Sales**: When the customer pays immediately.
- **Credit Sales**: When the customer will pay later.

Steps to Enter a Sales Voucher:

1. Go to **Gateway of Tally** > **Accounting Vouchers** > Press **F8 (Sales)**.
2. Select the type of invoice: **Item Invoice** or **Account Invoice**.
3. Enter the party's name (Customer).
4. Fill in inventory details (Stock Item, Quantity, Rate, etc.).
5. Apply any tax as needed (GST setup must be enabled).
6. Save the voucher using **Ctrl + A**.

Example:

Imagine your business sold 10 leather wallets at ₹500 each to a retail customer. Here's how the voucher looks:

- **Party A/c Name**: ABC Retail
- **Sales Ledger**: Sales @18% GST
- **Stock Item**: Leather Wallet
- **Qty**: 10
- **Rate**: ₹500
- **GST**: Auto-calculated

---

2. Understanding Purchase Vouchers

Purchase vouchers record the buying of goods or services from a supplier. Like sales, purchases can be on a cash or credit basis.

Types of Purchases:

- **Cash Purchase**: Payment made immediately.
- **Credit Purchase**: Payment to be made in the future.

Steps to Enter a Purchase Voucher:

1. Go to **Gateway of Tally** > **Accounting Vouchers** > Press **F9 (Purchase)**.
2. Choose the type of invoice.
3. Select the supplier.
4. Enter the items purchased with their rates and quantity.

5. Add GST or other applicable taxes.
6. Save the entry with **Ctrl + A**.

Example:

You purchase 100 notebooks from XYZ Stationers at ₹40 each:

- **Party A/c Name**: XYZ Stationers
- **Purchase Ledger**: Purchase @12% GST
- **Stock Item**: Notebook
- **Qty**: 100
- **Rate**: ₹40
- **GST**: Auto-calculated

3. Accounting Impact

Every sale or purchase entry affects at least two accounts:

- **Sales Entry**: Increases revenue, increases debtors (if on credit).
- **Purchase Entry**: Increases expenses or stock, increases creditors (if on credit).

This double-entry system ensures your books remain balanced and transparent.

4. Inventory Tracking

Sales and purchase vouchers also help maintain real-time inventory levels. When stock items are entered, Tally automatically deducts or adds the quantities to the inventory system.

5. GST in Sales & Purchases

For GST-registered businesses, proper tax classification is critical:

- **Sales Ledger**: Should be linked to a GST rate (e.g., Sales @18%).
- **Purchase Ledger**: Similarly, linked to a rate (e.g., Purchase @5%).

Tally ensures compliance by auto-calculating CGST, SGST, or IGST based on the party's location.

6. Tips for Effective Recording

- Use proper **naming conventions** for ledgers and stock items.
- Maintain **invoice numbers** and **reference numbers**.
- Set **credit limits** for customers and suppliers.
- Regularly **reconcile balances** with customer and supplier statements.

7. Common Mistakes to Avoid

- Selecting the wrong ledger (e.g., expense instead of sales).
- Not entering GST details for registered parties.
- Ignoring inventory details, leading to stock mismatches.
- Skipping narration, making audit trails unclear.

8. Practical Use-Case

Let's say your business receives a bulk order of school bags and supplies them to a local school:

- First, record the **purchase** of school bags using a purchase voucher.

- Next, create a **sales** voucher for the sale to the school.
- Tally will handle tax implications, update stock, and show net profit in reports.

Chapter 6: Inventory Management (Stock Groups, Items, Units)

Inventory is the backbone of every business dealing with physical goods. In Tally Prime, managing inventory accurately ensures smooth operations, accurate billing, and correct financial reporting. This chapter walks you through the core components of inventory management — stock groups, items, and units — along with real examples to give you a complete, practical understanding.

---

1. Why Inventory Management Matters in Business

Whether you run a supermarket, a manufacturing unit, or a wholesale business, tracking what you have, where it is, and how much it costs is vital. Poor inventory management can result in overstocking, stock-outs, or even financial discrepancies.

Tally Prime allows you to manage inventory in sync with your accounting data. This seamless integration ensures:

- Accurate billing
- Better inventory planning
- Real-time reporting
- Reduced losses

---

2. Stock Groups in Tally Prime

Definition: Stock Groups help you categorize stock items for better reporting and classification. Think of them like folders to organize your products.

Example:

- A business dealing in electronics might have stock groups like:
    - Mobile Phones
    - Laptops
    - Accessories

Steps to Create a Stock Group:

1. Gateway of Tally → Inventory Info → Stock Groups → Create
2. Enter the name (e.g., "Mobile Phones")
3. Select the parent group (Primary or another stock group)
4. Save

You can also enable 'Quantities to be added' if needed for internal tracking.

---

3. Stock Items in Tally Prime

Definition: A Stock Item represents a single product that you buy or sell. It's the smallest unit in your inventory system.

Example:

- iPhone 13 – 128 GB
- HP Laptop – 8GB RAM
- Samsung Earbuds

Steps to Create a Stock Item:

1. Gateway of Tally → Inventory Info → Stock Items → Create
2. Enter item name (e.g., "iPhone 13 – 128 GB")
3. Select stock group (e.g., "Mobile Phones")

4. Set unit of measurement (e.g., "Nos")
5. Enter opening balance if applicable

This helps in tracking:

- Opening stock
- Inward (purchases)
- Outward (sales)
- Closing balance

---

4. Units of Measurement

Definition: Units of Measurement (UOM) define the way you measure items. Common units include Nos (numbers), Kg, Ltr, Meter, etc.

Example:

- Nos for electronics
- Kg for grocery
- Mtr for textiles

Steps to Create Units of Measurement:

1. Gateway of Tally → Inventory Info → Units of Measurement → Create
2. Choose Simple (for one-to-one) or Compound (e.g., 1 Dozen = 12 Nos)
3. Enter symbol (e.g., Nos)
4. Save

Using proper units ensures:

- Uniformity in transactions
- Correct quantity calculation
- Reliable stock valuation

5. Inventory Management – In Practice

Let's say you own a small mobile shop.

- You create a stock group named "Mobile Phones"
- Then, you add items like "Samsung Galaxy S22", "Redmi Note 12", etc.
- Each item is assigned a unit "Nos"

Now, when you make a purchase entry, you choose the item, set quantity and rate, and it gets added to your stock. When you make a sales entry, the stock gets reduced.

6. Stock Summary Report

View Report: Gateway of Tally → Stock Summary

This report shows:

- Stock Item Name
- Opening Balance
- Inwards (purchases)
- Outwards (sales)
- Closing Stock

This is crucial for physical verification, reorder planning, and valuation.

7. Inventory with Batches and Expiry *(Optional)*

If you deal in perishable goods (like medicines), Tally allows batch-wise tracking with expiry dates. This can be enabled under inventory features.

Example:

- Paracetamol Batch A – Expiry: June 2026

---

8. Tips for Effective Inventory Management

- Avoid unnecessary stock groups — keep it simple.
- Use item codes for faster search.
- Periodically verify physical stock with Tally records.
- Regularly back up your data to prevent loss.

Chapter 7: GST in Tally – Setup, Invoicing & Returns

Introduction to GST in Tally Goods and Services Tax (GST) is an indirect tax levied on the supply of goods and services in India. Tally Prime, being a widely-used accounting software, is GST-ready and enables businesses to manage GST compliance efficiently. This chapter walks you through the complete process of configuring GST in Tally Prime, recording GST-compliant transactions, and generating returns.

7.1 Enabling GST in Tally Prime To use GST features in Tally, the first step is enabling GST in the company settings.

Steps to Enable GST:

1. Gateway of Tally > F11: Features > F3: Statutory & Taxation.
2. Set "Enable Goods and Services Tax (GST)" to Yes.
3. Set "Set/alter GST details" to Yes and press Enter.
4. Fill in your GSTIN, state, and applicable tax type (Regular, Composition, etc.).
5. Press Ctrl + A to save the configuration.

Pro Tip: Make sure your system date is set correctly. GST is applicable only for transactions on or after 1st July 2017.

7.2 Creating GST Ledgers You need to create separate ledgers for CGST, SGST, IGST, and Cess.

Example:

- CGST @ 9% (Group: Duties & Taxes, Type: GST)
- SGST @ 9%

- IGST @ 18%
- Cess @ 1% (if applicable)

This helps auto-calculate tax in vouchers and maintain accurate books.

7.3 Creating GST-Compliant Stock Items When creating stock items, it is important to define HSN/SAC codes and applicable GST rates.

Steps:

1. Gateway of Tally > Inventory Info > Stock Items > Create.
2. Enter item details.
3. Under GST Details, specify the HSN code and applicable rate.

Example:

- Item: Laptop
- HSN Code: 8471
- GST Rate: 18%

7.4 Creating GST-Registered Parties Customer and supplier masters must include GSTIN and state details.

Steps:

1. Gateway of Tally > Accounts Info > Ledgers > Create.
2. Under Statutory Details, fill in GST registration type and GSTIN.

This ensures that Tally applies the correct type of tax—CGST+SGST or IGST—based on the party's state.

7.5 Recording GST Transactions Tally supports GST for different types of vouchers:

Sales Voucher:

- Gateway of Tally > Accounting Vouchers > F8: Sales.
- Select customer, items, quantity, rate.
- Tax will auto-apply based on item and party.

Purchase Voucher:

- Gateway of Tally > Accounting Vouchers > F9: Purchase.
- Enter details of your purchase.
- GST is auto-calculated.

Example: You sell a laptop worth ₹50,000 to a customer in the same state.

- CGST @ 9% = ₹4,500
- SGST @ 9% = ₹4,500
- Total Invoice = ₹59,000

7.6 GST Reports & Returns in Tally Tally generates multiple GST reports to help businesses file returns:

View Reports:

- Gateway of Tally > Display > Statutory Reports > GST.

Reports Available:

- GSTR-1 (Outward Supplies)

- GSTR-2A (Inward Supplies auto-populated)
- GSTR-3B (Summary Return)
- GST Computation (Tax payable/receivable)

Filing Tip: Export your GSTR data from Tally and upload it to the GST Portal via offline tools.

7.7 GST Adjustment Entries Sometimes, manual adjustments are needed:

Examples:

- Rounding-off taxes
- Writing off GST difference
- Adjustment of excess ITC

Tally allows journal entries for such cases using GST Adjustment accounts.

7.8 GST Compliance Checklist

- Always use updated Tally Prime version.
- Ensure accurate HSN/SAC codes.
- Maintain party GSTIN correctly.
- Regularly check for errors in GST reports.

Chapter 8: Bank Reconciliation & Cheque Management

In business accounting, ensuring that your books match your actual bank transactions is crucial for maintaining accuracy and credibility. This is where **Bank Reconciliation** comes in. Tally Prime makes it easy for businesses to reconcile bank accounts and manage cheque transactions effectively. Let's explore how this is done and why it matters.

1. What is Bank Reconciliation?

Bank Reconciliation is the process of matching the balance in your company's accounting records (Tally) with the corresponding information on a bank statement. The goal is to find and explain any differences between the two records.

Example:

If Tally shows a closing bank balance of ₹1,00,000 but your bank statement shows ₹95,000, the ₹5,000 difference might be due to uncleared cheques or bank charges not recorded in Tally.

2. Importance of Bank Reconciliation

- Ensures accounting accuracy
- Identifies errors and frauds
- Tracks unpresented cheques and bank charges
- Builds trust with auditors and stakeholders

3. Steps to Reconcile a Bank Statement in Tally Prime

a. Open the Bank Ledger:

- Go to **Gateway of Tally > Display More Reports > Account Books > Ledger**

- Select the desired bank account

b. Enter the Bank Statement Date:

- Press **F5** for reconciliation mode

- Enter the date from the actual bank statement

c. Match Transactions:

- Tally displays a list of bank entries

- Enter the cheque/date of deposit for each transaction as per your bank statement

Tally automatically calculates the balance and shows unreconciled entries.

d. Save the Reconciliation:

- Once all matching entries are updated with their dates, Tally will show a reconciled balance.

---

4. Common Reasons for Differences

- Cheques issued but not presented

- Deposits in transit
- Bank charges or interest not recorded
- Errors in data entry

5. Managing Cheques in Tally

Handling cheques properly is a key part of accounting. Tally allows you to track issued and received cheques efficiently.

a. Recording Cheque Payments:

When issuing a cheque:

- Use **Payment Voucher (F5)**
- Enter bank name, cheque number, and date
- Mention party account and amount

b. Recording Cheque Receipts:

When receiving a cheque:

- Use **Receipt Voucher (F6)**
- Enter the same details (party, cheque number, bank, date)

c. Cheque Bounce / Dishonour:

- Use **Journal Voucher (F7)** to reverse the receipt entry
- Debit the party account and credit the bank

6. Post-dated Cheques (PDC) Management

Tally Prime supports **Post-dated Vouchers**, helpful in recording cheques that are dated for future.

How to Record:

- Press **Ctrl+T** while creating a voucher to mark it as a post-dated voucher
- Tally will include it in reports only after the date arrives

7. Bank Reconciliation Report

Tally provides a report for quick analysis of reconciled and unreconciled entries:

- Go to **Gateway of Tally > Banking > Bank Reconciliation**
- Select the bank and view details

This report helps you identify missing entries, delays in cheque clearances, and pending deposits.

8. Best Practices for Bank Reconciliation & Cheque Management

- Reconcile monthly or weekly for active accounts
- Maintain clear naming for parties and vouchers
- Regularly update cheque status
- Train accounting staff for consistency
- Review reconciliation report before closing books monthly

9. Real-Life Example

Let's say your business issued a cheque of ₹20,000 to a vendor on 25th March, but it was presented to the bank on 2nd April. During March bank reconciliation:

- The cheque appears in Tally but not on the bank statement
- You'll mark the cheque as uncleared in March and update it in April reconciliation

Chapter 9: Payroll in Tally – Salary Structure, Employee Records

Managing employee payroll is a crucial aspect of every business operation. Tally Prime simplifies this by offering an integrated payroll system that allows businesses to automate salary processing, maintain employee records, and ensure compliance with statutory regulations. This chapter explores the key features and step-by-step processes for setting up and managing payroll in Tally.

---

1. Understanding Payroll in Tally

Payroll in Tally enables users to define employee profiles, assign salary structures, record attendance, calculate statutory deductions, and generate payslips and reports. It is especially useful for small to medium businesses aiming to streamline their HR and accounting functions.

---

2. Enabling Payroll Feature

To begin using payroll in Tally Prime:

- Go to **Gateway of Tally > F11: Features > F1: Accounting Features**
- Set **'Maintain Payroll'** to **Yes**
- Accept the configuration

This activates the payroll module and adds payroll-related options to the menu.

---

3. Creating Employee Masters

1. Navigate to **Gateway of Tally > Payroll Info > Employees > Create**

2. Enter the employee's **name**, **date of joining**, **designation**, and **group** (e.g., Staff, Managerial)
3. You can create individual employees or use the **Employee Groups** feature to organize them.

Example:

- Name: Ravi Sharma
- Department: Accounts
- Designation: Accountant
- Date of Joining: 01-April-2024

---

4. Creating Pay Heads

Pay Heads represent individual salary components like basic pay, allowances, deductions, etc.

1. Go to **Payroll Info > Pay Heads > Create**
2. Define Pay Head Name (e.g., Basic Salary)
3. Type of Pay Head: **Earnings for Employees** / **Deductions from Employees**
4. Under Income Type, choose **Fixed** or **Attendance Based**
5. Link to accounts for ledger classification

Examples of Pay Heads:

- Basic Pay
- House Rent Allowance (HRA)
- Provident Fund (PF)
- Professional Tax (PT)

- Bonus

5. Creating Salary Structure (Payroll Category)

You can define the salary structure using a **Payroll Category** to organize pay heads assigned to employees.

1. Go to **Payroll Info > Salary Details > Create**
2. Select the employee or group
3. Add the necessary Pay Heads and their respective values

Example Salary Structure for an Employee:

- Basic: ₹20,000
- HRA: ₹5,000
- Conveyance: ₹1,500
- PF Deduction: ₹2,000
- Professional Tax: ₹200

6. Processing Payroll

Once employees and salary details are added, monthly salary processing is easy:

1. Navigate to **Gateway of Tally > Payroll Vouchers > Ctrl + F4: Payroll**
2. Select the month and employee
3. Tally auto-populates salary based on assigned structure
4. Save the voucher to complete payroll processing

7. Attendance & Leave Management

Tally also allows attendance tracking:

- Create Attendance/Production Types (e.g., Present, Leave, Half-day)
- Record attendance for employees
- Link pay heads to attendance (for variable earnings)

This ensures salary is calculated based on presence or shifts.

8. Generating Payslips

To provide employees with payslips:

- Go to **Display** > **Payroll Reports** > **Payslip**
- Choose the month and employee
- View, print or export as PDF

Payslips contain a breakup of earnings, deductions, net pay, and statutory details.

9. Statutory Compliance in Payroll

Tally supports calculation and reporting for:

- **Provident Fund (PF)**
- **Employee State Insurance (ESI)**
- **Professional Tax (PT)**
- **Income Tax (TDS)**

These are configurable under Payroll Statutory options and can be linked to specific pay heads.

10. Payroll Reports in Tally

Useful payroll reports include:

- Paysheet
- Salary Register
- Employee Pay Head Breakup
- Attendance Sheet
- Gratuity Report

These reports support audits and business decisions.

11. Real Business Scenario Example

Case: A startup has five employees and wants to pay them based on fixed salary and attendance. The accountant uses Tally to:

- Create employee profiles
- Define pay heads for salary and PF
- Link attendance to salary
- Process salaries each month and print payslips

This saves hours of manual work and ensures compliance.

Chapter 10: TDS & TCS in Tally

Introduction

Tax Deducted at Source (TDS) and Tax Collected at Source (TCS) are vital components of the Indian taxation system. Tally Prime offers an integrated module for managing both TDS and TCS transactions. This chapter explains how businesses can automate and accurately manage TDS/TCS-related accounting entries in Tally.

What is TDS?

TDS (Tax Deducted at Source) is a method where the person responsible for making certain payments such as salary, commission, rent, etc., deducts tax before making the payment to the recipient and deposits it with the government.

Examples of TDS:

- TDS on salary
- TDS on rent payments above ₹50,000 per month
- TDS on contractor payments

What is TCS?

TCS (Tax Collected at Source) is the tax collected by the seller from the buyer at the time of sale of specified goods and services.

Examples of TCS:

- Sale of scrap

- Sale of minerals like coal, lignite, iron ore
- Sale of motor vehicle exceeding ₹10 lakh

Enabling TDS in Tally Prime

Step-by-Step:

1. Go to **F11: Features** > **Statutory & Taxation**.
2. Enable **TDS**.
3. Set/alter TDS details: Yes.

Fill in:

- TAN Number
- Deductor Type (Company/Individual etc.)
- Responsible Person's Details

Creating TDS Nature of Payment:

Gateway of Tally > **Accounts Info** > **Statutory Info** > **TDS Nature of Payment** > Create

Example: Rent – 10% under Section 194I

Creating Ledgers for TDS

1. **Expense Ledger** (e.g., Rent):

    - Under: Indirect Expenses
    - Set Is TDS Applicable: Yes
    - Select Nature of Payment: Rent

2. **TDS Ledger**:

    - Under: Duties & Taxes
    - Type of Duty: TDS
    - Nature of Payment: Rent

3. **Party Ledger** (Vendor/Supplier):

    - Under: Sundry Creditors
    - Maintain balances: Yes
    - Is TDS Deductable: Yes

Booking a TDS Transaction

Go to **Accounting Vouchers** > **F5: Payment**

Example:

You pay ₹50,000 as office rent.

TDS @ 10% = ₹5,000

- Rent Expense: ₹45,000
- TDS Payable: ₹5,000
- Bank/Cash: ₹50,000

TDS Reports in Tally

Gateway of Tally > Display More Reports > Statutory Reports > TDS Reports

Types:

- TDS Computation
- Deductee Ledger
- Challan Reconciliation
- Form 26Q & 27Q Generation

Enabling TCS in Tally Prime

Step-by-Step:

1. Gateway of Tally > **F11: Features** > **Statutory & Taxation**
2. Enable TCS: Yes
3. Set TCS details: Yes

Fill in:

- Collector Type
- PAN/TAN number
- Collection Category (e.g., scrap, minerals)

Creating TCS Ledgers

1. **Sales Ledger**:

    - Under: Sales
    - Is TCS Applicable: Yes
    - Select Nature of Goods: Scrap

2. **TCS Ledger**:
    - Under: Duties & Taxes
    - Type of Duty: TCS
    - Nature of Collection: Scrap @ 1%
3. **Customer Ledger**:
    - Under: Sundry Debtors
    - Is TCS Applicable: Yes

Recording a TCS Transaction

Example: You sell scrap worth ₹1,00,000 TCS @ 1% = ₹1,000

Sales Voucher:

- Scrap Sales: ₹1,00,000
- TCS Collected: ₹1,000
- Total Invoice: ₹1,01,000

TCS Reports in Tally

Gateway of Tally > Display More Reports > Statutory Reports > TCS Reports

- TCS Computation
- Collector Ledger
- Form 27EQ generation

Compliance Reminders

- File TDS returns on time (Form 26Q, 24Q)
- File TCS returns quarterly using Form 27EQ
- Validate TDS/TCS challans and maintain acknowledgment numbers
- Issue TDS/TCS certificates to deductees/collectees (Form 16A/27D)

Common Mistakes to Avoid

- Not deducting TDS on time
- Deducting wrong rates
- Mismatched TAN or PAN in returns
- Late deposit of TDS/TCS causing penalties

Chapter 11: Multi-Currency, Cost Centres & Budgets

In today's global and diversified business environment, companies frequently operate across borders and departments. Efficiently managing financial transactions in multiple currencies and tracking departmental performance is essential for business accuracy and growth. Tally Prime offers robust features for Multi-Currency handling, Cost Centre allocations, and Budget controls. This chapter explores these features in-depth and provides real-world examples to enhance understanding and usability.

---

1. Understanding Multi-Currency in Tally

1.1 Why Multi-Currency is Important

Businesses that deal with international clients or suppliers often receive or pay money in different currencies. Accurate conversion, recording, and reporting of such transactions is crucial.

1.2 Enabling Multi-Currency in Tally

To use Multi-Currency:

- Go to **Gateway of Tally > F11: Features > Accounting Features**
- Set **Enable Multi-Currency** to 'Yes'

1.3 Creating a New Currency

Steps:

- Go to **Gateway of Tally > Accounts Info > Currencies > Create**

- Enter the details:
    - **Symbol**: e.g., USD
    - **Formal Name**: US Dollar
    - **ISO Currency Code**: USD
    - **Number of Decimal Places**: 2
    - **Conversion Rate**: e.g., 1 USD = 83 INR

1.4 Using Currency in Transactions

When creating or altering ledgers for parties (like customers or vendors), you can assign a default currency. During voucher entry, Tally will auto-convert amounts based on the current exchange rate.

Example:

You invoice a US client for $1000. If the exchange rate is 1 USD = 83 INR, the invoice is recorded as INR 83,000. Tally keeps both currency values in reports.

---

2. Cost Centres in Tally

2.1 What are Cost Centres?

Cost Centres are used to track expenses and incomes department-wise or project-wise.

2.2 Enabling Cost Centres

- Go to **F11 > Accounting Features**
- Enable **Cost Centres and Cost Categories**

2.3 Creating Cost Centres

- Go to **Accounts Info > Cost Centres > Create**
- Name: e.g., Marketing, Sales, Production
- Assign under Primary

2.4 Allocating Cost Centres in Transactions

When passing a voucher:

- Enter amount > Tally will prompt **Cost Centre Allocation screen**
- Assign portions to specific centres

Example:

Salary expense of Rs. 1,00,000 is split:

- Marketing: Rs. 40,000
- Sales: Rs. 60,000

This allocation helps generate department-wise profitability and cost analysis.

---

3. Budgeting in Tally

3.1 Why Use Budgets?

Budgets help control expenses and compare actual performance against projected figures.

3.2 Enabling Budgets

Budgets can be applied to:

- Ledgers (e.g., Office Supplies)
- Cost Centres (e.g., Marketing Dept.)

3.3 Creating Budgets

- Go to **Accounts Info > Budgets > Create**
- Name: FY 2025 Marketing Budget
- Period: Start and End date
- Select Ledger or Cost Centre
- Enter budgeted amounts monthly or yearly

3.4 Monitoring Budgets

Go to **Display > Statements of Accounts > Budget Variance** to compare actual vs. budgeted figures.

Example:

Marketing budget is Rs. 1,00,000 but actual spending is Rs. 1,30,000. The Budget Variance report will show a Rs. 30,000 overrun.

---

4. Real-Life Application Scenario

Case Study: Export Firm

ABC Exports receives payments from US and UK clients in USD and GBP. They also manage sales and support teams and allocate salaries and expenses accordingly. Tally's multi-currency feature helps maintain accurate accounts, while Cost Centres separate departmental expenses. They use Budgets to forecast and control marketing spend.

Benefits:

- Transparent financial planning
- Efficient departmental management
- Easy multi-currency handling without manual conversion

5. Summary

Tally Prime's Multi-Currency, Cost Centres, and Budgets functionalities empower businesses to operate seamlessly in complex environments. These tools ensure transparency, help in performance tracking, and support financial discipline.

Next Steps:

- Practice creating multiple currencies
- Allocate expenses via Cost Centres
- Monitor performance through Budgets

Mastering these features will not only make you proficient in Tally but also give you real-world accounting control skills highly valued in modern businesses.

Chapter 12: Generating MIS Reports (P&L, Balance Sheet, Stock Summary)

In today's competitive business landscape, decision-making needs to be fast, data-driven, and accurate. That's where **MIS (Management Information System) Reports** come into play. Tally Prime offers powerful MIS capabilities that help in generating insightful reports such as Profit and Loss Account, Balance Sheet, and Stock Summary. These reports provide a snapshot of the financial health of a business and guide owners and managers in strategic planning.

1. What is MIS Reporting?

MIS Reports in Tally provide essential data analytics and summaries of a business's activities. These reports are auto-generated based on the transactions recorded in Tally and help in tracking performance, spotting trends, and making informed business decisions.

2. Profit & Loss Account in Tally

The **Profit & Loss (P&L)** account is a financial statement that summarizes revenues, costs, and expenses over a specific period. It shows the net profit or loss of a company.

Steps to View P&L in Tally:

1. From the Gateway of Tally, go to **Reports > Profit & Loss A/c**.
2. You'll see two columns — one for income and one for expenses.
3. Net profit or loss will be automatically calculated and shown at the bottom.

Customization Tips:

- Press F2 to change the period.
- Use F1 to toggle between detailed and condensed view.
- Use F12 for configuration, such as including opening balances or showing vertical formats.

Example:

Let's say a business earns revenue from sales worth ₹5,00,000 and incurs expenses (purchase, rent, salaries) of ₹3,50,000. The P&L will show a net profit of ₹1,50,000.

3. Balance Sheet in Tally

A **Balance Sheet** gives a snapshot of the company's financial position — what it owns and what it owes — on a particular date.

Steps to View Balance Sheet:

1. Go to **Gateway of Tally > Reports > Balance Sheet**.
2. You'll see two sections:
    - **Liabilities**: Capital, loans, sundry creditors
    - **Assets**: Cash/bank, stock, fixed assets

Features:

- Press F12 to customize display (e.g., show profit/loss in liabilities).
- Drill down to each ledger for deeper analysis.

Real-Life Relevance:

Investors and lenders often look at the balance sheet before funding or partnering with a company.

---

4. Stock Summary Report

The **Stock Summary** report provides details of available stock, quantities, rates, and stock value based on different valuation methods.

Steps to View Stock Summary:

1. Go to **Gateway of Tally > Reports > Stock Summary**.
2. You'll see item-wise closing balances, quantity, rate, and value.

Benefits:

- Tracks inventory performance
- Highlights slow-moving or fast-moving items
- Helps with reorder planning

Example:

If you have 100 units of Item A at ₹50 each and 200 units of Item B at ₹30 each, your stock value is ₹11,000. Stock Summary gives you this information instantly.

---

5. Exporting Reports

You can export all these reports to PDF or Excel for sharing or auditing purposes.

Steps:

- Press Ctrl + E while viewing any report
- Choose format (PDF/Excel)
- Set the destination path

6. How These Reports Help Businesses

- **P&L Account** helps in understanding business profitability
- **Balance Sheet** gives insights into financial strength
- **Stock Summary** helps optimize inventory and reduce dead stock

These reports also help in:

- Filing tax returns
- Applying for loans
- Planning expansions
- Identifying cost-saving opportunities

7. Tips for Effective Reporting

- Regularly reconcile ledgers to avoid wrong reports
- Maintain proper stock entries for accuracy
- Use cost centers for departmental reporting

Conclusion

MIS reporting in Tally is not just about numbers — it's about making those numbers meaningful. With just a few clicks, you get insights that take hours to compile manually. These reports transform accounting data into valuable business intelligence. Whether you're a small startup or a growing enterprise, mastering MIS reporting can elevate your business strategy.

Chapter 13: Backup, Restore & Data Security in Tally

In the realm of business accounting, data is everything. From customer records to inventory details, sales transactions to payroll — every single byte of information holds critical importance. Tally Prime, being a comprehensive business management software, recognizes this and offers robust features to ensure that your financial data is not only well-organized but also secure and recoverable. In this chapter, we dive into how to effectively manage backups, restore company data, and implement security measures within Tally to safeguard sensitive information.

13.1 Importance of Data Backup

Before diving into the how-to, let's understand **why** backups are essential.

- **Protection from accidental deletion:** A user might unintentionally delete vital data or a company altogether.

- **System failure or corruption:** Hardware malfunctions, power outages, or viruses can corrupt your data.

- **Migration & portability:** Backups are often required when shifting data from one system to another.

- **Audit or reference purposes:** Old backups serve as reference points during audits.

Example: Imagine a retail chain's accountant accidentally deletes the current year's company file. Without a recent backup, the business could lose months of work.

13.2 How to Backup Data in Tally Prime

Backing up in Tally Prime is simple and takes just a few steps:

Step-by-Step Process:

1. **Open Tally Prime**
2. From the **Gateway of Tally**, press Alt + Y to open the **Data Menu.**
3. Select **Backup.**
4. In the **Source Path**, select the folder where your data is currently stored (usually by default C:\TallyPrime\Data).
5. In the **Destination Path**, choose where you want to store your backup (e.g., D:\TallyBackup\).
6. Select the company you want to back up.
7. Press Enter to confirm and complete the backup.

Best Practices:

- Use an **external hard drive** or **cloud storage** for additional protection.

- Schedule backups **weekly or monthly**, depending on the transaction volume.

Real-World Tip: Use Google Drive, Dropbox, or OneDrive to store Tally backups. Create a zipped folder for each backup by date (e.g., Company_ABC_2025-05-01.zip).

13.3 Restoring Data in Tally Prime

Restoring a backup is essentially retrieving data from your previously saved backup file.

Steps to Restore:

1. Launch **Tally Prime.**
2. Press Alt + Y > **Restore.**
3. In the **Source Path,** enter the path where the backup is located.
4. In the **Destination Path,** provide the data location in Tally (usually C:\TallyPrime\Data).
5. Select the backup you want to restore.
6. Hit Enter to begin the restoration.

Note: Ensure no company is active when restoring.

Common Use-Case:

Let's say your computer was formatted, and Tally was reinstalled. You can restore the backup and resume work as if nothing changed.

13.4 Data Security in Tally

Tally provides **user-level access control**, **password protection**, and **audit features** to safeguard data.

A. Password Protection

- You can set **admin and user-level passwords.**

- To activate security control:

  - Go to Gateway of Tally > F11 > F3 (Company Features)

  - Set **Use Security Control** to Yes

  - Assign usernames and passwords with access rights

B. User Roles and Access

- Tally allows defining multiple user roles:
  - **Data Entry Operator**: Can only enter vouchers.
  - **Manager**: Can access reports but not modify ledgers.
  - **Auditor/Admin**: Full access.

Scenario: In a medium-sized firm, the accountant handles daily entries, while the manager views sales reports, and only the owner can modify master settings.

C. Data Encryption

Though basic encryption is handled by Windows, businesses can use third-party tools or secure drives for extra protection.

13.5 Auto Backup Feature (Tally Prime Edit Log)

Tally Prime also supports **Edit Log** and **Auto Backup** (in Gold versions or with Tally Server).

Benefits:

- Automatically saves backup copies at fixed intervals
- Tracks every change made — who made it and when
- Useful for audits and large teams

13.6 Exporting Data for Backup

Tally also allows exporting data in XML or Excel format:

- Go to any report (e.g., Ledger)
- Press Alt + E to Export
- Choose **Format**: Excel, PDF, XML, JSON

This is useful for:

- Sharing specific reports with stakeholders
- Backing up just a part of your data (e.g., ledger or sales)

13.7 Common Mistakes to Avoid

1. **Not backing up regularly**
2. **Storing backups on the same device** (which can fail)
3. **Using weak or no passwords**
4. **Not testing restore before it's needed**
5. **Ignoring audit trails in shared systems**

Chapter 14: Shortcut Keys & Customization

In the fast-paced world of digital accounting and business management, speed and efficiency can make all the difference. Tally Prime, known for its intuitive design, also provides a wide range of shortcut keys and customization options that enhance user experience, improve data entry accuracy, and save time. In this chapter, we will explore the most essential Tally shortcut keys along with practical examples and walk through the steps for interface customization to suit specific business needs.

Section 1: Why Shortcut Keys Matter in Tally

Imagine being able to complete a full day's work in half the time. That's what mastering shortcut keys in Tally can do. These key combinations reduce dependence on the mouse, allowing users to focus entirely on keyboard-based navigation.

Benefits of Using Shortcut Keys:

- Increases speed of data entry
- Reduces fatigue from repetitive mouse usage
- Minimizes errors
- Boosts productivity during high-volume transaction entries

Section 2: Commonly Used Tally Shortcut Keys

Below is a list of vital Tally shortcut keys categorized by their use cases:

Navigation & Windows Control:

- **Alt + F1** – Close a company or view detailed report
- **Alt + F3** – Company Info menu
- **Ctrl + A** – Accept a form or screen
- **Ctrl + Q** – Quit from a screen

Voucher Entry:

- **F4** – Contra Voucher
- **F5** – Payment Voucher
- **F6** – Receipt Voucher
- **F7** – Journal Voucher
- **F8** – Sales Voucher
- **F9** – Purchase Voucher

Master Creation/Alteration:

- **Alt + C** – Create a new master while entering a transaction
- **Ctrl + Enter** – Alter a master from voucher screen

Reports & Printing:

- **Alt + P** – Print
- **Alt + E** – Export
- **Alt + M** – Email
- **Alt + I** – Insert a voucher
- **Alt + D** – Delete a voucher or master

Inventory:

- **Alt + G** – Display Stock Summary
- **F11** – Company Features
- **F12** – Configuration

Section 3: Practical Examples of Using Shortcut Keys

Scenario 1: You're entering a Sales Voucher. Instead of using the mouse:

1. Press **F8** to open the Sales Voucher.
2. Use **Alt + C** to create a new item or ledger on the fly.
3. Use **Ctrl + A** to quickly accept the voucher.

Scenario 2: While checking the stock status:

1. Press **Alt + G** to open Stock Summary.
2. Drill down using **Enter** to review stock movement.

These small actions multiplied over a day save hours of time.

Section 4: Customization in Tally Prime

Every business operates differently. Customization ensures Tally adapts to the workflow rather than the other way around.

1. Tally Configuration (F12):

Tally provides a menu called Configuration where users can customize data input forms, reports, appearance, inventory, statutory features, etc.

Example:

- Disable unnecessary fields to simplify voucher entry.
- Enable batch-wise details or expiry dates for inventory tracking.

2. Company Features (F11):

Company Features allow enabling/disabling features like:

- GST
- Cost Centres
- Payroll
- Multi-Currency

Example:

- A company using only cash transactions can disable banking options to simplify the interface.

3. Display Customization:

- Use color schemes and columnar formats for better visual clarity.
- Save views for repeated reports.

4. Security Controls:

- Customize user roles with specific access to ledgers, vouchers, or features.

Section 5: Advanced Customization using TDL (Tally Definition Language)

For businesses with specific needs, Tally provides a scripting environment via TDL.

- Create custom fields (e.g., agent code, vehicle number)
- Design special reports (e.g., aging summary, region-wise sales)

Note: TDL requires technical knowledge or hiring a Tally developer.

Conclusion

Shortcut keys and customization are the secret sauces that turn a regular Tally user into a power user. They improve performance, reduce chances of error, and align the software perfectly with business needs. From speeding up voucher entry with a single keystroke to tailoring Tally's interface for your unique workflows, mastering these tools is essential for any student, entrepreneur, or accounting professional looking to get the best out of Tally Prime.

By making these small but impactful changes, you not only save time but build confidence and fluency in the world of digital accounting.

Pro Tip: Practice using three new shortcut keys every day for a week. By the end, you'll feel like a Tally ninja!

Chapter 15: Mini Projects – Practical Business Scenarios

In this chapter, we bring together everything you've learned in Tally by presenting real-world mini projects. These projects simulate practical business situations and allow you to apply accounting, inventory, payroll, GST, and reporting knowledge within Tally Prime.

Project 1: Small Retail Shop Setup

Scenario: You are managing a local garment store.

Tasks:

- Create a new company in Tally Prime.
- Create ledgers for customers, suppliers, sales, and purchases.
- Create stock items like shirts, trousers, jeans, etc., with units and stock groups.
- Enter purchase and sales vouchers.
- Apply 5% GST on both purchase and sale.
- Generate stock summary, P&L, and balance sheet.

Learning Outcome: This helps you understand inventory handling and GST implementation for a small trading business.

Project 2: Freelance Graphic Designer

Scenario: You are an individual offering design services.

Tasks:

- Create ledgers for client income, software subscription expenses, and freelance income.
- Enter journal vouchers for service charges received.
- Apply GST (18%) where applicable.
- Track payments received via UPI or bank.
- Generate GST invoice and expense report.

Learning Outcome: Gain hands-on experience in service-based accounting and income reporting.

Project 3: Manufacturing Unit (Custom Furniture)

Scenario: You run a small-scale furniture manufacturing unit.

Tasks:

- Define stock items for raw materials and finished goods.
- Configure bill of materials (BOM).
- Record consumption of raw materials and creation of finished goods.
- Use journal entries for production.
- Record sales with GST.

Learning Outcome: Learn production tracking, material management, and inventory conversion in Tally.

Project 4: Payroll Management in a Consultancy Firm

Scenario: You handle HR and finance for a consultancy with 5 employees.

Tasks:

- Create employee master records.
- Define pay heads (Basic, HRA, DA, PF).
- Process monthly salaries.
- Record statutory deductions like PF & TDS.
- Generate payslips and payroll summary.

Learning Outcome: Understand employee salary setup and payroll processing inside Tally.

Project 5: Multi-Branch Business

Scenario: You manage accounting for a business with 3 branches.

Tasks:

- Enable cost centres.
- Create separate cost centres for each branch.
- Record incomes and expenses branch-wise.
- Generate cost centre reports to compare branch performance.

Learning Outcome: Learn cost centre configuration and profitability comparison.

www.ingramcontent.com/pod-product-compliance
Lightning Source LLC
LaVergne TN
LVHW022021200926
848481LV00007B/2471